THE WONDER BOOK OF
TREES

By CYNTHIA ILIFF KOEHLER
and ALVIN KOEHLER

WONDER BOOKS • NEW YORK

MAPLE

CHESTNUT

SYCAMORE

HORSE
CHESTNUT

SPRUCE

OAK

This jar of seeds could make a whole forest.

There are many sizes and shapes of tree seeds. A maple tree seed is of one particular size and shape — and only a maple tree will grow from it. A chestnut tree seed is another particular size and shape — and only a chestnut tree will grow from it.

LINDEN

AILANTHUS

POPLAR

Tree seeds travel about. Some have "wings" and are carried off by the wind. Others have "propellers" to help them fly away. And a few are thrown off from the mother tree when their pods explode.

FLOWERS

SEEDS

WITCH HAZEL

CATALPA

SWEET GUM

Animals help carry tree seeds to new places where they can grow. Seeds in berries are often carried off by hungry birds.

Squirrels bury seeds for food and sometimes forget to come back for them. And some seeds are in burrs which stick to the fur of animals.

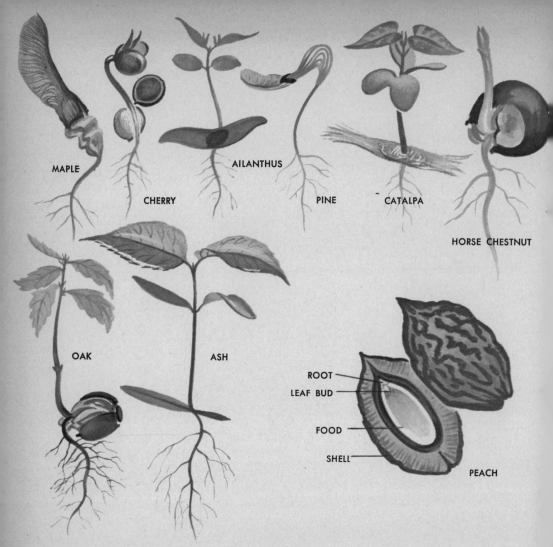

MAPLE

CHERRY

AILANTHUS

PINE

CATALPA

HORSE CHESTNUT

OAK

ASH

ROOT

LEAF BUD

FOOD

SHELL

PEACH

Every seed is a tiny package of food with a speck of sleeping plant at one end. When the seed is warm and moist, a tiny root reaches down into the earth and a stem shoots up toward the sun. The young tree lives on the food in the seed until it has grown its first leaves.

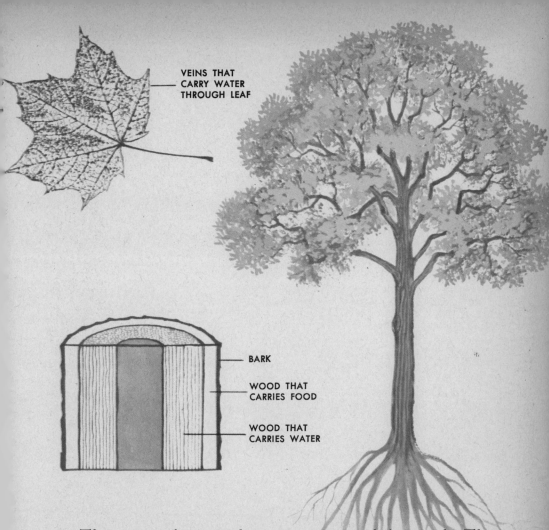

VEINS THAT
CARRY WATER
THROUGH LEAF

BARK

WOOD THAT
CARRIES FOOD

WOOD THAT
CARRIES WATER

The roots of a tree draw water out of the earth. The stem or trunk is like a bundle of straws. The straws take the water from the roots up to the leaves. Using green chlorophyll, which gives them their color, the leaves combine the water with sunlight and air. In a wonderful way they make food for the tree.

WILLOW   ELM   BIRCH   OAK

HORSE CHESTNUT   SPRUCE   POPLAR   AILANTHUS   MAPLE

When trees are crowded together in a forest, they reach high up for the light. But when trees grow with open space around them, they grow in different shapes. Some point up like spears. Others droop like fountains. There are some which spread out like fans, and still others which look more like balls. See how many shapes you can learn to recognize.

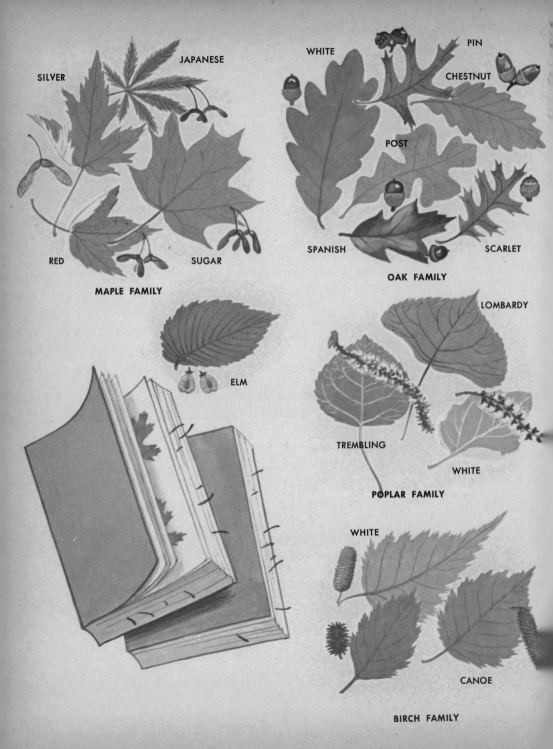

SILVER

JAPANESE

RED

SUGAR

MAPLE FAMILY

WHITE

PIN

CHESTNUT

POST

SPANISH

SCARLET

OAK FAMILY

ELM

LOMBARDY

TREMBLING

WHITE

POPLAR FAMILY

WHITE

CANOE

BIRCH FAMILY

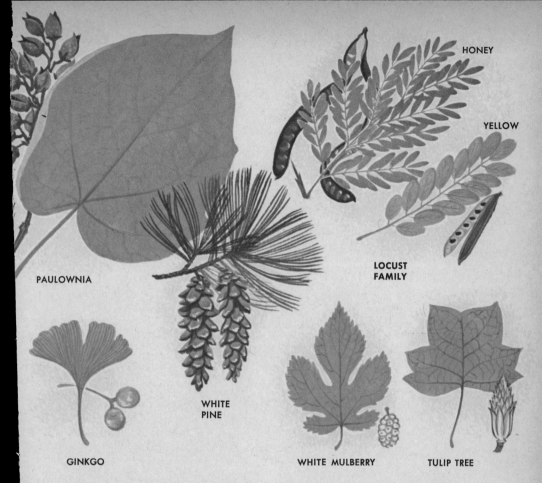

HONEY

YELLOW

LOCUST
FAMILY

PAULOWNIA

WHITE
PINE

GINKGO

WHITE MULBERRY

TULIP TREE

If you gather the leaves of different kinds of trees to press them in a book, you will find that there are many different shapes, and you may need more than one book. Some are as small as pins and others as large as dinner plates.

There are different families of trees, such as the oaks or maples or birches. If you look at the leaves and seeds of a tree, you usually can tell to what family they belong.

Gather a bunch of twigs in the winter. At the tip and along the stem you will see little bumps. These bumps are sleeping buds.

If you put your tree buds in water in a warm house, you will see them begin to swell and open. Underneath the covering of a bud is a whole year's growth of leaves and stem, and maybe even a flower. If you cut a big bud in half, you can see just how this is.

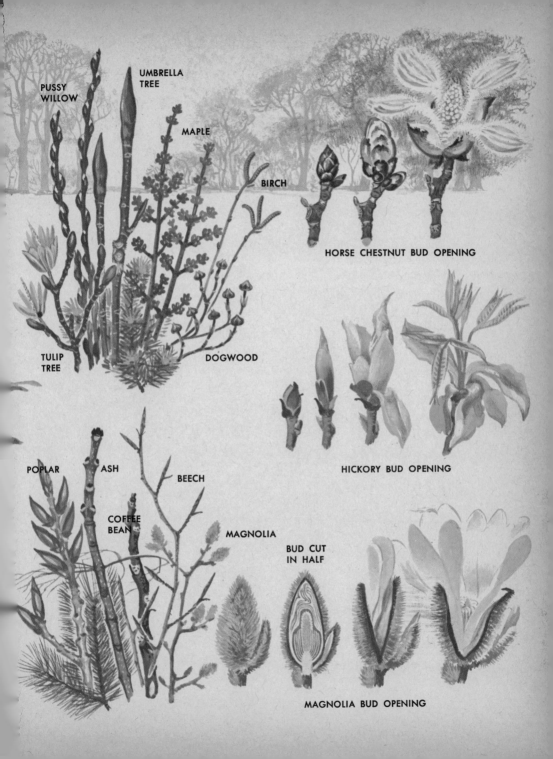

PUSSY
WILLOW

UMBRELLA
TREE

MAPLE

BIRCH

HORSE CHESTNUT BUD OPENING

TULIP
TREE

DOGWOOD

HICKORY BUD OPENING

POPLAR

ASH

BEECH

COFFEE
BEAN

MAGNOLIA

BUD CUT
IN HALF

MAGNOLIA BUD OPENING

MAGNOLIA

TULIP TREE

PAULOWNIA

PAWPAW

YELLOW
LOCUST

PLUM

MAGNOLIA

Do you hurry by the trees or do you stop to look?
Have you noticed in the spring what kind of flowers
each tree has? Every tree has flowers. Some are big like
the magnolia or dogwood. But there are other flowers
that are not so easy to see.

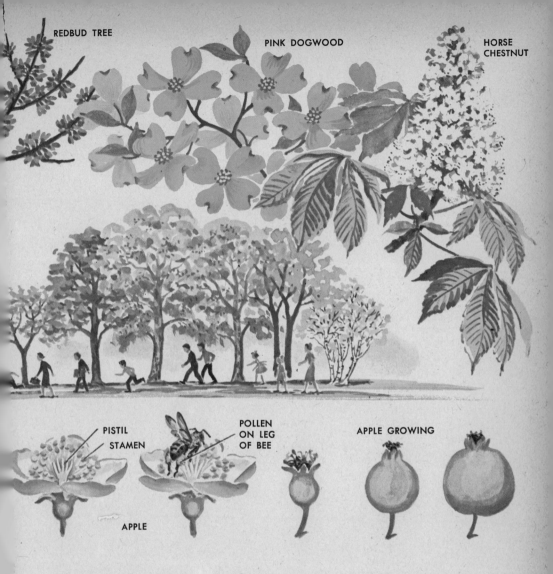

REDBUD TREE

PINK DOGWOOD

HORSE CHESTNUT

PISTIL
STAMEN

POLLEN
ON LEG
OF BEE

APPLE GROWING

APPLE

Most trees have one kind of flower with two important parts — the stamens, which have a dust called pollen, and the pistil, which makes the seed when the pollen dust is brought to it by the wind or by insects.

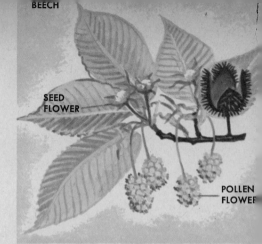

BEECH

SEED
FLOWER

POLLEN
FLOWER

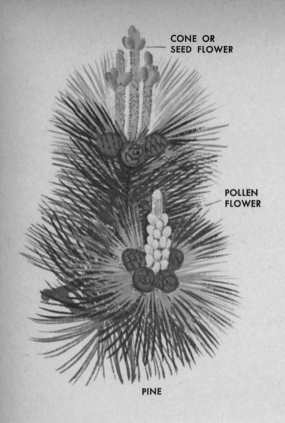

CONE OR
SEED FLOWER

POLLEN
FLOWER

PINE

HORNBEAM

POLLEN
FLOWER

SEED
FLOWER

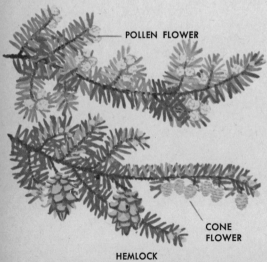

POLLEN FLOWER

CONE
FLOWER

HEMLOCK

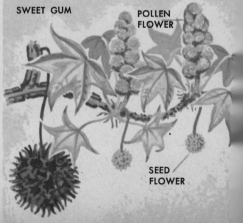

SWEET GUM

POLLEN
FLOWER

SEED
FLOWER

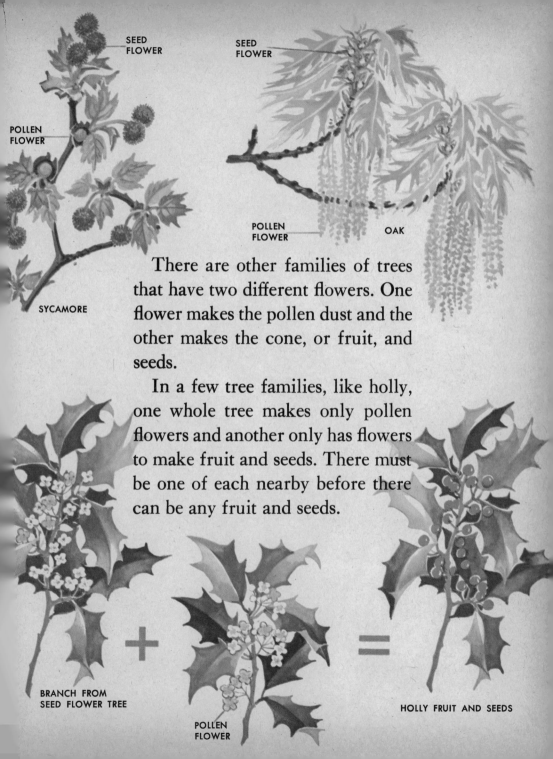

SEED FLOWER

SEED FLOWER

POLLEN FLOWER

POLLEN FLOWER

OAK

SYCAMORE

There are other families of trees that have two different flowers. One flower makes the pollen dust and the other makes the cone, or fruit, and seeds.

In a few tree families, like holly, one whole tree makes only pollen flowers and another only has flowers to make fruit and seeds. There must be one of each nearby before there can be any fruit and seeds.

BRANCH FROM SEED FLOWER TREE

+

POLLEN FLOWER

=

HOLLY FRUIT AND SEEDS

Some trees are called evergreens because they are green both in summer and in winter. They drop old needles and grow new ones a few at a time. The old needles make a brown carpet under the trees.

Other trees lose their leaves in the fall. All summer the leaves are busy making food so that the tree can live and grow bigger. The food is stored in the seeds and in the little buds that will live through the winter. When summer's work is done, the green chlorophyll in the leaves disappears and suddenly there are bright colors everywhere.

What would the world ever do without trees? Where would birds build their nests or a raccoon hide her cubs? We wouldn't have pears or apples or walnuts. Houses, boats, chairs, tables, pencils, violins and matches — not to mention shade and beauty — are all made from trees.